This is Pat.

Pat has a cat.
It is a fat cat.

The cat has a nap
on Pat's hat.
It is a bad cat.

Pat ran to the cat.

The cat ran to Pat's dad.

Pat is mad with the cat.
It sat on Pat's hat.

Pat's dad is not mad
with the cat.

Pat's dad has the cat on his lap.

Pat is mad with Dad and she cannot get the cat.

Pat is upset. Pat is sad.
She cannot get the cat
and she has not got a hat.

The cat is not upset.
The cat is on Dad's lap.

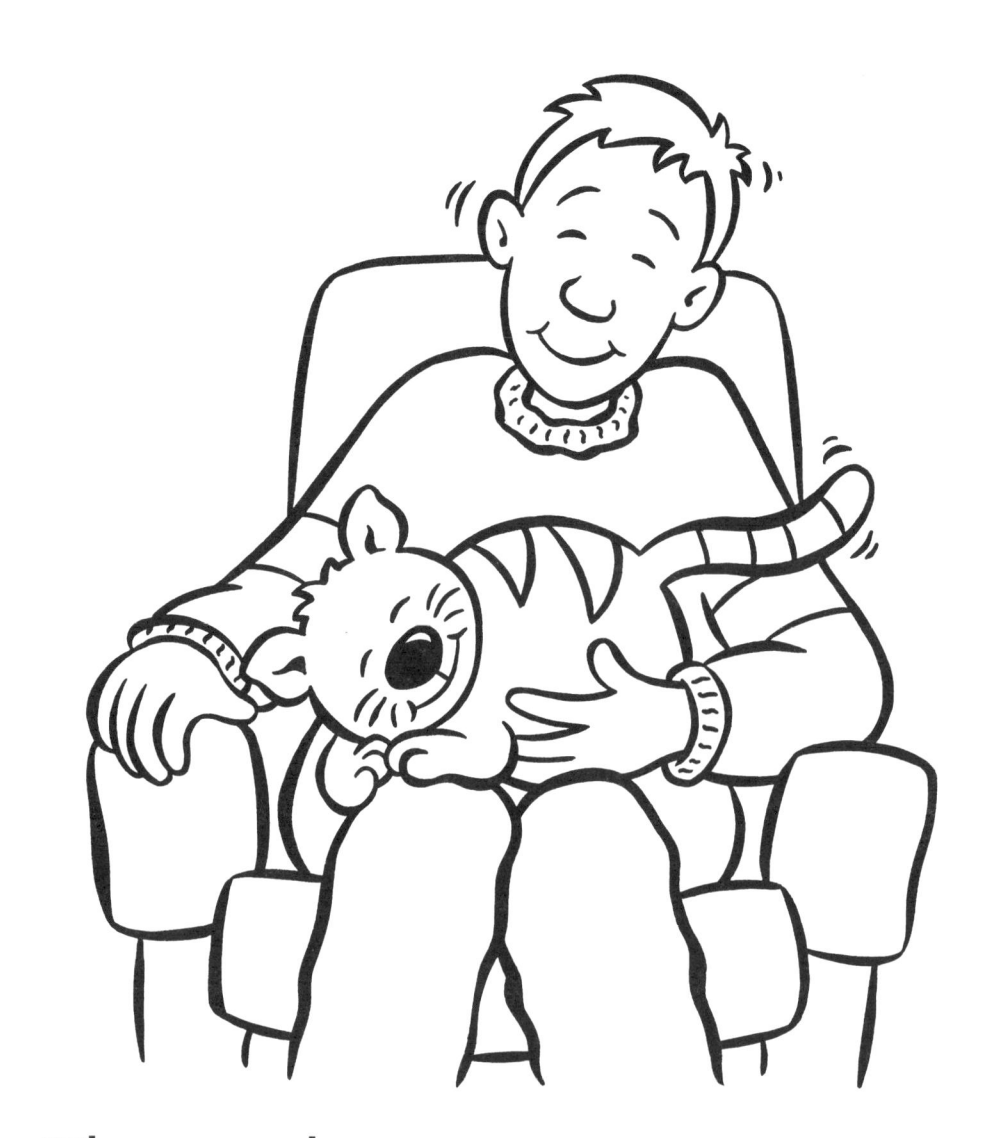

The cat has a nap
on Dad's lap.